ARACHNID WORLD

WIND SCORPIONS

SANDRA MARKLE

KILLER JAWS

LERNER PUBLICATIONS COMPANY MINNEAPOLIS

FOR CURIOUS KIDS EVERYWHERE

ACKNOWLEDGMENTS

The author would like to thank Mr. Warren Savary, California Academy of Sciences, and
Dr. Simon Pollard, Canterbury Museum, Christchurch, New Zealand, for sharing their
expertise and enthusiasm. A special thanks to Skip Jeffery for his support during the
creation of this book.

Lerner Publications Company
A division of Lerner Publishing Group, Inc.
241 First Avenue North
Minneapolis, MN 55401 U.S.A.

Website address: www.lernerbooks.com

Library of Congress Cataloging-in-Publication Data

Markle, Sandra.
    Wind scorpions : killer jaws / by Sandra Markle.
      p.   cm. — (Arachnid world)
    Includes bibliographical references and index.
    ISBN 978–0–7613–5048–4 (lib. bdg. : alk. paper)
    1. Solpugida—Juvenile literature. I. Title.
  QL458.8.M37 2012
  595.4'8—dc23   2011021599

Manufactured in the United States of America
1 - DP - 12/31/11

CONTENTS

AN ARACHNID'S WORLD

WELCOME TO THE WORLD OF ARACHNIDS

(ah-RACK-nidz). Arachnids can be found in every habitat on Earth except in the deep ocean. Some are even found in Antarctica.

So how can you tell if an animal is an arachnid rather than a relative like the insect shown below? Both belong to a group of animals called arthropods (AR-throh-podz). All animals in this group share some traits. They have bodies divided into segments, jointed legs, and a stiff exoskeleton. This is a skeleton on the outside like a suit of armor. But one way to tell if an animal is an arachnid is to count its legs and main body parts. While not every adult arachnid has eight legs, most do. Arachnids also have two main body parts. Adult insects, like the staghorn beetle *(right)*, have six legs and three main body parts. Some insects may also have wings. Arachnids never have wings.

This book is about arachnids called wind scorpions. Wind scorpions have big, strong jaws. They can kill prey that would seem too big for them to tackle *(facing page)*. Their jaws also allow them to defend against other predators (hunters).

WIND SCORPION FACT

A wind
scorpion's
body temperature
rises and falls with the
temperature around it.
It must warm up to
be active.

NOT A SPIDER OR A SCORPION

Wind scorpions are sometimes called camel spiders or sun spiders. These arachnids are unique. They're neither spiders nor scorpions. Spiders spin silk. They use their silk to catch prey and defend themselves. Spiders also have fangs and bite to inject venom (liquid poison). Scorpions catch prey and defend themselves with pincerlike pedipalps (leglike parts). A scorpion also has a stinger-tipped tail and flicks it to inject venom.

Wind scorpions don't spin silk. They don't have fangs, a stinger, or pincerlike pedipalps. They also don't produce venom. To catch prey and stay safe, wind scorpions have giant jaws—the biggest of any arachnid.

WIND SCORPION

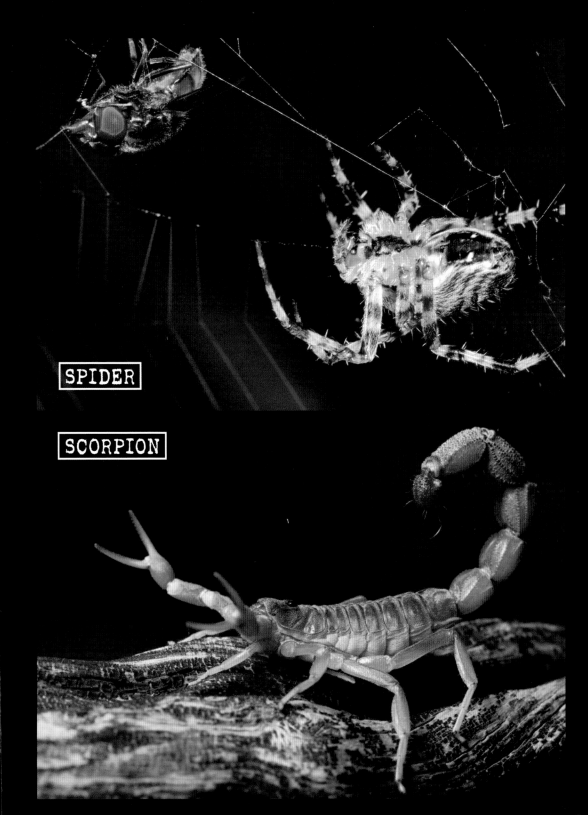

SPIDER

SCORPION

MIGHTY JAWS

A wind scorpion's big jaws are also called chelicerae (keh-LIH-seh-ree). They stick out in front and make up about one-third of its total body length. A large part of the chelicerae is muscle. Unlike human jaws, the right and left side of a wind scorpion's jaws move separately.

The upper and lower parts of each chelicera have sharp, pointed teeth. The upper part stays in place. Muscles move the lower part up to meet it. This makes for a powerful pinch, almost like a nutcracker. The bite of a wind scorpion *(right)* is powerful enough to break through skin or scales. A wind scorpion's jaws are strong enough to break through an exoskeleton too. The wind scorpion's jaws tear into the soft tissue underneath. Then the upper and lower jaws work together to crush and grind.

WIND SCORPION FACT

While a wind scorpion's bite won't make a human sick, it will hurt. The wound will need to be cleaned to prevent infection.

ON THE OUTSIDE

There are more than one thousand different kinds of wind scorpions. Besides powerful jaws, they all share certain features. First, they have two main body parts: the cephalothorax (sef-uh-loh-THOR-ax) and the abdomen. The exoskeleton is made up of many hard plates connected by stretchy tissue. This lets the wind scorpion bend and move. Check out other key features most wind scorpions share.

LEGS:
These are used for walking, climbing, and digging. The underside of each of the last pair of legs has five fan-shaped sensory organs called the racquet organs.

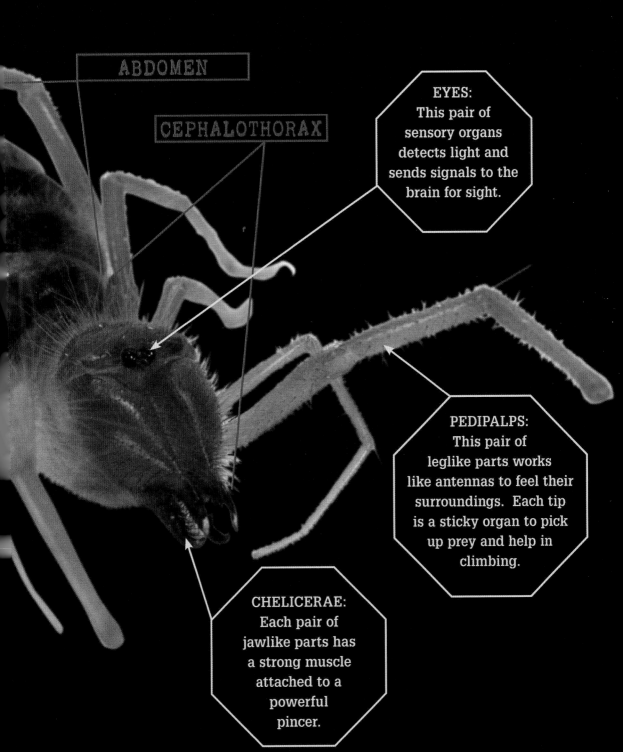

ABDOMEN

CEPHALOTHORAX

EYES:
This pair of sensory organs detects light and sends signals to the brain for sight.

PEDIPALPS:
This pair of leglike parts works like antennas to feel their surroundings. Each tip is a sticky organ to pick up prey and help in climbing.

CHELICERAE:
Each pair of jawlike parts has a strong muscle attached to a powerful pincer.

ON THE INSIDE

Look inside an adult female wind scorpion.

BRAIN: This organ sends and receives messages to and from body parts.

MALPIGHIAN (MAHL-pig-ee-an) TUBULES: This is a system of tubes that cleans the blood of wastes.

ESOPHAGUS: A tube through which liquid food passes on the way to the pharynx.

COXAL (KAHK-sehl) GLAND: Special groups of cells that collect liquid wastes and pass them through openings to the outside.

MIDGUT: An organ whose juices continue the process of digestion.

SPERMATHECA (spur-muh-THEE-kuh): A sac where sperm is stored after mating.

PHARNYX (FAR-inks): This muscular tube contracts and expands to pump food into the midgut. Its hairs filter out hard waste bits.

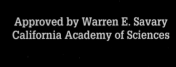

Approved by Warren E. Savary
California Academy of Sciences

CAECA (SEE-kuh): Branching tubes that store liquid food.

HEART: This muscular tube pumps blood toward the head. Then blood flows throughout the body and back to the heart.

HINDGUT: An organ that stores food and passes nutrients to the blood.

STERCORAL (STER-kor-uhl) POCKET: This is a place where wastes collect before passing out of the body.

NERVE GANGLIA: These bundles of nerve tissue send messages between the brain and other body parts.

TRACHEAE (TRAY-kee-ee): Three pairs of tubes that let in air and move oxygen throughout the body.

OVARY: This organ produces eggs for reproduction.

BECOMING ADULTS

Like all arachnids, baby wind scorpions become adults through incomplete metamorphosis (meh-tuh-MOR-fuh-sis). *Metamorphosis* means "change." A wind scorpion's life includes three stages: egg, immature, and adult. An immature goes through a number of stages, called instars, before it becomes an adult. An immature *Galeodes* (gay-lee-OH-deez) is tiny enough to perch on a fingertip.

SOME KINDS OF ARTHROPODS GO THROUGH COMPLETE METAMORPHOSIS. The four stages are egg, larva, pupa, and adult. Each stage looks and behaves very differently.

IMMATURE

Compare the immature *Galeodes* to the adult below. The adult's body is about 2 inches (5 centimeters) long. Its leg span is about 5 inches (12 cm). The immature's coloring is different too. The immature and the adult look different. But the immature can do anything the adult can do except mate and produce young.

WIND SCORPION FACT

A wind scorpion's long back legs have more segments than those of other arachnids. That makes them extra flexible and helps them run fast—some say as fast as the wind. That's how they got their nickname.

ADULT

Wind scorpion immatures survive on their own because their mothers give them a good start. When a female wind scorpion, like the *Eremobates* (air-ee-moh-BAY-teez), is ready to lay her eggs, she begins to burrow *(below)*. She uses her sturdy second and third pairs of legs and her jaws to dig into the soil. She digs until she has a burrow big enough to hide inside.

The number of eggs females lay depends on the kind of wind scorpion. It also depends on whether she's been able to catch enough big prey to gain the energy she needs to produce eggs. Most female wind scorpions, like the *Branchia* (BRAN-kee-uh) below, lay between twenty and eighty eggs. The mother stays with the eggs. She guards them from predators such as scorpions and wolf spiders. Depending on the kind of wind scorpion, it takes a few days to more than a month for the young to hatch.

Newborn wind scorpions, like the *Eremobates* at right, are called first instars. They look and behave differently from older immatures. That's because first instar wind scorpions aren't fully developed. Their legs don't work well enough for them to walk. Their chelicerae don't work well enough for them to catch prey or eat.

When the wind scorpions were developing inside their eggs, they ate the egg's yolk (stored food) to provide the energy they needed to grow. The first instars eat the remaining yolk just before they hatch. This provides energy for them to continue developing for about a week. During this time, their mother stays with them. Just by being there, she helps keep them safe from predators.

About a week later, the young wind scorpions molt (shed their exoskeleton). Then they're ready to hunt prey and to feed themselves. And they'll be able to sense predators in time to run away.

WIND SCORPION FACT

When young wind scorpions molt, their exoskeletons split open. They have a soft, new exoskeleton underneath. The heart pumps blood to swell the body and stretch the exoskeleton. The new exoskeleton will harden later. The stretched exoskeleton allows the young wind scorpion room to grow before it has to molt again.

FIRST INSTAR

EGG

19

WHAT'S OUT THERE?

To catch prey, some kinds of arachnids sit still. Wind scorpions go hunting. They are well equipped to sense anything moving around them—prey or predators. All wind scorpions have long hairlike sensors on their bodies *(right)*. Some have so many they look furry. The sensors feel tiny ground movements and air currents. A wind scorpion can tell when something is moving nearby and how close it is. It can also judge whether what's moving is prey-sized or big enough to be a threat.

WIND SCORPION FACT

Some kinds of wind scorpions live in grasslands and forests. But most live in dry regions the world over, except for Australia. Those that live in hot deserts also have a coat of fine hairs. These act as a layer protecting their bodies from the drying heat.

Wind scorpions have five tiny, fan-shaped flaps, called racquet organs, on each of their back legs. As a wind scorpion walks or runs, it taps the ground with its back legs. The racquet organs feel bits of matter on anything they touch. Wind scorpions also have little pits on their front pair of legs. These hold more sensors. This wind scorpion *(right)* located the grasshopper using its sensors.

Wind scorpions have two large eyes. They let the wind scorpion tell light from dark and make out shapes. They help the wind scorpion avoid objects in its path. Sight also helps the wind scorpion judge when and where to bite its prey.

EYES

GET A GRIP

Wind scorpions like the *Galeodes* below have another feature they rely on—their pedipalps. These look like extra long legs, and they do help wind scorpions get around. However, unlike their legs, the pedipalps don't end in claws. The tip is a sticky organ made up of tiny ridges. These give the wind scorpion a good grip on smooth surfaces. When this tip organ isn't needed, the wind scorpion pulls it inside its body. The wind scorpion can pull the sticky organ to just below the surface of the pedipalp to keep it clean and safe.

WIND SCORPION FACT

Wind scorpions can climb glass!

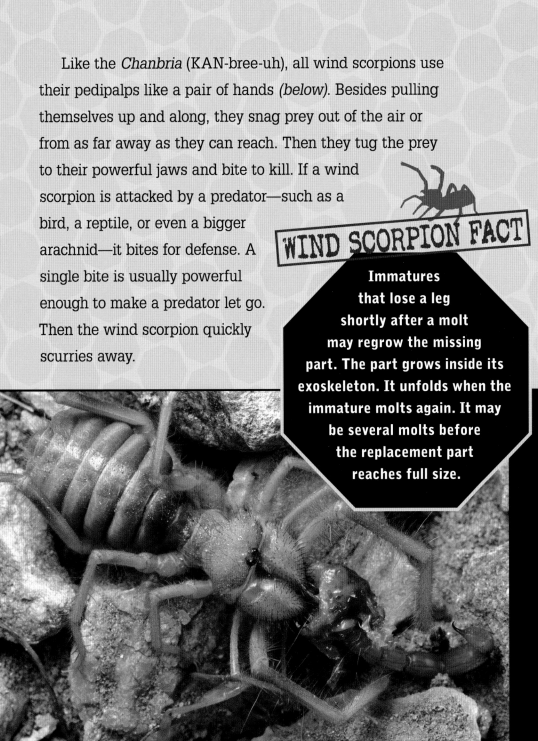

Like the *Chanbria* (KAN-bree-uh), all wind scorpions use their pedipalps like a pair of hands *(below)*. Besides pulling themselves up and along, they snag prey out of the air or from as far away as they can reach. Then they tug the prey to their powerful jaws and bite to kill. If a wind scorpion is attacked by a predator—such as a bird, a reptile, or even a bigger arachnid—it bites for defense. A single bite is usually powerful enough to make a predator let go. Then the wind scorpion quickly scurries away.

WIND SCORPION FACT

Immatures that lose a leg shortly after a molt may regrow the missing part. The part grows inside its exoskeleton. It unfolds when the immature molts again. It may be several molts before the replacement part reaches full size.

A HUNTING LIFE

Just as the sun is rising in Israel's Negev Desert, the male *Galeodes* digs a burrow and crawls inside. There he rests from the sun's drying heat. When he senses the air cooling again, he leaves his burrow and scurries across the sand. He's hunting. His body uses up food energy quickly, so he needs to eat every day. He doesn't always find prey, but tonight his racquet organs quickly pick up the trail of a wolf spider.

WIND SCORPION FACT

For a few seconds, wind scorpions are able to run about 20 inches (53 cm) per second—about 1 mile (1.6 kilometers) per hour.

He follows this track until his sensory hairs tell him something prey-sized is moving close by. He charges. Like all wind scorpions, the male *Galeodes* can run fast for short bursts. Wolf spiders are fast too. But the wind scorpion wins this race. He snags his prey with his pedipalps. Pulling the spider close, the *Galeodes* bites to make the kill.

Next, the male *Galeodes* tears off chunks of the spider and grinds these up with his powerful jaws *(right).* As he does this, digestive juices pour out of his mouth onto his food. These juices dissolve the prey's soft tissues. The wind scorpion sucks in this soupy liquid. He repeats the process until only hard bits of the spider's exoskeleton remain.

COURTING DANGER

If the male *Galeodes* fails to find prey for a night or two, he moves to a new area. One night, after moving to a new burrow, he molts for the final time. Now, he's a mature male ready to mate.

When he picks up the trail of a female *Galeodes*, he tracks her. As he gets close, he goes very slowly. If she's not ready to mate, she'll run away. Or she will rear up, wave her front legs, and open her chelicerae—her defense display. A female that isn't ready to mate may kill the male. A courting male must be ready to make a quick getaway.

MALE

WIND SCORPION FACT

Male wind scorpions will only mate with their own kind of female wind scorpion.

FEMALE

The male *Galeodes* moves close enough to touch the female with his pedipalps. She stops moving and stays still. Then the male charges forward *(right)*. He grabs the female with his chelicerae and bends her abdomen over her cephalothorax. Next, he deposits a spermatophore on the ground. This is a compact mass of sperm—the male reproductive cells. He picks up the mass with his chelicerae and pushes it into the female's gonopore, her reproductive opening.

When mating is over, the male hurries away. If he's able to find another female, he'll mate again before he dies. Most males and females live for no more than a year.

THE CYCLE CONTINUES

Shortly after the male leaves, the female *Galeodes* moves on, hunting for prey. With a body about 2 inches (5 cm) long, she's as big as she'll get. She's also big enough to catch larger prey than ever before. When her sensors tell her a lizard is close by, she tracks it.

Finally, she's close enough to actually see her prey. She sprints the final distance and grabs the lizard with her pedipalps. The female *Galeodes* begins to eat even before the lizard is dead.

WIND SCORPION FACT

Stretchy tissues connect the sections of a wind scorpion's exoskeleton so its abdomen can expand during a big meal.

During the day, the female *Galeodes* seeks shelter in a burrow to escape the drying heat. Every night, she hunts. Over the next week, eggs develop inside her body until her abdomen is swollen with them *(right)*. Finally, she's ready to lay them. She settles into her burrow for a longer than usual stay.

One by one, as each egg moves out of her body, the egg joins with a sperm (male reproductive cell). The female has been storing the sperm since she mated. Once egg and sperm join, a tough capsule forms around the outside of the egg.

The female lays almost one hundred eggs. She stays with them in the burrow. When a wolf spider comes close, searching for a meal, the female darts out. She attacks and eats the wolf spider. This way, she keeps her eggs safe and gains energy for her guard duty.

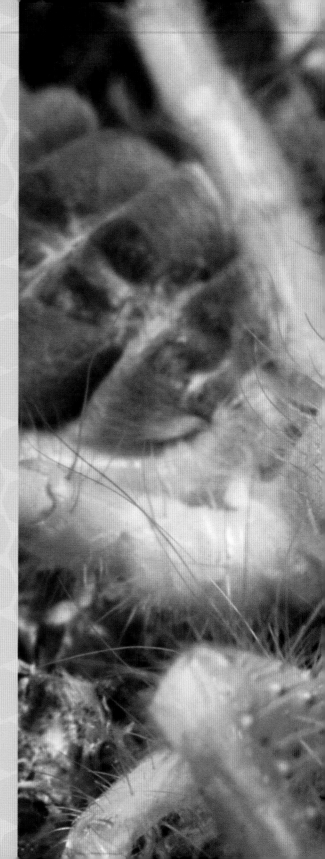

In just a few days, the first instars hatch. At first, their exoskeletons are soft. They don't have sensory hairs. The instars can't support themselves on their legs or use their jaws. The female stays with her young for another week until they molt. She doesn't care for her offspring. Still, by being with them, she protects them from predators.

After they molt, the immatures can walk and use their jaws. They're ready to take care of themselves. Once the immatures leave the burrow, the female goes hunting again. But her life cycle is complete. After a few more weeks, the female *Galeodes* dies.

The immatures hunt tiny prey and grow bigger. Many immature *Galeodes* become prey themselves. Bigger predators, such as scorpions, catch and eat the immature *Galeodes*.

The immature *Galeodes* that do survive catch and eat prey to grow. They continue to grow and molt for almost a year before becoming adults.

Male *Galeodes* that find a female *Galeodes* mate. Then the female produces eggs, digs a burrow, and lays her eggs. She guards them, and after they hatch, she guards the first instars. The young molt, and armed with powerful jaws, they continue the wind scorpion's life cycle.

WIND SCORPIONS AND OTHER BIG-JAWED ARACHNIDS

WIND SCORPIONS BELONG TO A GROUP, or order, of arachnids called Solifugae (SOLE-ee-FEW-jee). There are eleven hundred different kinds of these arachnids. Scientists sometimes also call Solifugae Solifugids.

SCIENTISTS GROUP living and extinct animals with others that are similar. So wind scorpions are classified this way:

> kingdom: Animalia
> phylum: Arthropoda
> class: Arachnida
> order: Solifugae

HELPFUL OR HARMFUL? Wind scorpions are both. They're helpful because they eat a lot of insects. They help control the numbers of insect pests. They're harmful because they bite when touched. This bite can be very painful. The bite should be cleaned with a powerful liquid to prevent infection.

HOW BIG IS a wind scorpion? The body of an adult *Galeodes* is about 2 inches (5 cm) long.

MORE BIG-JAWED ARACHNIDS

Compare how a wind scorpion uses its big jaws to the way these arachnids use their big jaws.

Long-jawed orb weavers live all over the world. Both males and

females of this kind of orb weaver spider have extra long jaws. Even though their bodies are shorter, the males have the longer jaws. During mating, the pair lock jaws. This may keep the female from attacking—even killing—the male. After mating, the male guards the female. He uses his big jaws to fight and drive off other males. That's because the last male to mate with the female before she lays her eggs is the father of all her offspring.

Pantopsalis luna are a type of harvestman that live in New Zealand.

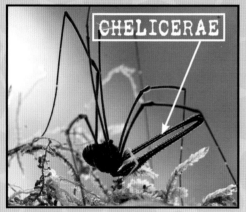

They have long chelicerae as well as long legs. The jaws of the male are much longer than those of the female. The jaws also end in crablike pincers. *Pantopsalis luna* often scavenge the remains of dead arthropods. With their long pincer jaws, the males break open the exoskeleton of big flies to eat the muscle inside. The bigger the jaws, the bigger the flies they can break open. Because males allow females to feed with them, females are attracted to males with the biggest chelicerae.

abdomen: the rear end of an arachnid. It contains systems for digestion and reproduction.

adult: the reproductive stage of an arachnid's life cycle

brain: the organ that sends and receives messages from body parts

caecae: branches of the digestive system where liquid food is stored

cephalothorax: the front end of an arachnid. It includes the mouth, the brain, and the eyes. Legs are also attached to this part.

chelicerae: a pair of jawlike parts that stick out near the mouth. In wind scorpions, these have large muscles attached to sharp-tipped pincers that have teeth on the inner edge.

egg: a female reproductive cell; also the name given to the first stage of an arachnid's life cycle

esophagus: a tube through which food passes on the way to the pharynx

exoskeleton: a protective, armorlike covering on the outside of the body

eyes: sensory organs that detect light and send signals to the brain for sight. Wind scorpions have two large eyes in the middle of the head.

gonopore: the female reproductive opening

heart: a muscular tube that pumps blood toward the head. Blood eventually flows throughout the body and back to the heart.

hindgut: an organ through which food nutrients pass into the blood and are carried throughout the body

immature: a juvenile wind scorpion that can do everything an adult can do except mate and produce offspring

instar: a newly hatched, immature wind scorpion

legs: body extensions used for walking, climbing, and burrowing

Malpighian tubules: a system of tubes that cleans the blood of wastes

midgut: an organ through which digestive juices pour to continue digestion

molt: to shed the exoskeleton

nerve ganglia: bundles of nerve tissue that send messages between the brain and other body parts

ovary: the body part that produces eggs

pedipalps: a pair of long, leglike body parts on either side of the mouth. In wind scorpions, they have a sticky organ at the tip to catch prey and assist in climbing. They are also covered with sensory hairs and are used like antennae to help the wind scorpion feel its way.

pharynx: a muscular body part that contracts to create a pumping force, drawing food into the body's digestive system. Hairs filter out hard waste bits.

predator: an animal that catches and kills other animals, its prey, to survive

prey: animals caught by predators

racquet organs: sensory organs that detect bits of matter on anything they touch

sperm: the male reproductive cell

spermatheca: a sac in the female where sperm is stored after mating

spermatophore: a compact mass of male reproductive cells

stercoral pocket: a place where wastes collect before passing out of the body

tracheae: tubes that move oxygen throughout the body

DIGGING DEEPER

To keep on investigating wind scorpions, explore these books and online sites.

BOOKS

Bishop, Nic. *Nic Bishop Spiders*. New York: Scholastic, 2007. Amazing photos illustrate an amazing variety of arachnids.

Markle, Sandra. *Outside and Inside Spiders*. New York: Aladdin, 1999. Read about how an arachnid's body works to help it survive.

Murphy, Julie. *Arachnids: Weird, Wild, and Wonderful*. New York: Gareth Stevens, 2010. Look at different kinds of arachnids, the wind scorpion's close relatives.

Walker, Richard. *One Million Things: Animal Life*. New York: DK Publishing, 2009. A survey in text and photos gives information about all members of the animal kingdom including arachnids.

MORE FROM SANDRA MARKLE

ARACHNID WORLD:

Black Widows

Harvestmen

Orb Weavers

Scorpions

Ticks

Wolf Spiders

WEBSITES

BBC: Creepiest Creature: Solifugids

http://www.bbc.co.uk/nature/life/Solifugae#p009cpz4

This video shares an exciting look at key features, especially the jaws, of solifugids.

Empire of the Camel Spider

http://video.clipstream.com/content/c/camel_spiders/

Don't miss the video showing this arachnid in action, burrowing and catching scorpion prey.

National Geographic: Big Bite

http://ngm.nationalgeographic.com/ngm/0407/feature5/index.html

See great close-up photos. Discover interesting facts. Find out what it was like to photograph these interesting arachnids in their natural habitat.

Visit www.lernerresource.com for free, downloadable arachnid diagrams, research assignments to use with this series, and additional information about arachnid scientific names.

WIND SCORPION ACTIVITY

All wind scorpions have a sticky organ on the tip of each of their two long pedipalps. Try this activity to see one way wind scorpions use this organ to eat.

1. Work with an adult partner to pop a cup of popcorn.

2. Place a piece of waxed paper on the table in front of you. Scatter the popped corn on the waxed paper.

3. Wash and dry your hands. Roll a thumbnail-sized ball of peanut butter dough (see recipe below) between your hands until it's soft. Press it onto one end of a plastic straw.

4. Sit at the table in front of the scattered popcorn.

5. Touch the peanut butter ball to one piece of popped corn. Press down lightly. Lift. The popcorn should stick.

6. Lift it to your mouth. Carefully pick the popcorn off with your teeth and eat.

7. Repeat.

This activity gives you a feel for how wind scorpions pick up little prey, such as termites. The pedipalps bend to move the prey to its killer jaws.

Peanut Butter Dough

¼ cup creamy peanut butter
¼ cup instant powdered milk
2 tablespoons honey

Put all ingredients in a bowl. Mix with a spoon until a soft dough forms. After completing the activity, mix the remaining dough with raisins, roll into balls, and enjoy this tasty treat.

INDEX

PHOTO ACKNOWLEDGMENTS

The images in this book are used with the permission of: © Simon Pollard, pp. 4, 41 (bottom);
© Mark Moffett/Minden Pictures, pp. 5, 14, 17, 24, 25, 28–29, 30–31; © OSF/M. Fogden/
Animals Animals, p. 6; © Jef Meul/Minden Pictures, p. 7 (top); © Roger de la Harpe/Gallo
Images/Getty Images, p. 7 (bottom); © Joe Warfel/Eighth-Eye Photography, pp. 8–9, 16,
21; © Kim Taylor/naturepl.com, pp. 10–11, 22–23; © Laura Westlund/Independent Picture
Service, pp. 12–13; © Peter Chadwick/Photo Researchers, Inc., p. 15; © Warren E. Savary,
pp. 19, 34–35; © Francesco Tomasinelli/Natural Visions, p. 27; © Francesco Tomasinelli/
Photo Researchers, Inc., p. 33; © OSF/D. Fox/Animals Animals, pp. 36–37; © David Hosking/
Minden Pictures, pp. 38–39; © Ken Preston-Mafham/Premaphotos, p. 41 (top); © Piotr
Naskrecki/Minden Pictures, p. 47.

Front cover: © Michael Fogden/Oxford Scientific/Getty Images.

Main body text set in Glypha LT Std 55 Roman 12/20. Typeface provided by Adobe Systems.